Teaching Writing in the Content Areas:

ELEMENTARY SCHOOL

Stephen N. Tchudi
and
Susan J. Tchudi

National Education Association
Washington, D.C.

Printing History
 First Printing: September 1983
 Second Printing: August 1984
 Third Printing: July 1985
 Fourth Printing: December 1987
 Fifth Printing: October 1989

Note

The opinions expressed in this publication should not be construed as representing the policy or position of the National Education Association. Materials published as part of the Writing in the Content Areas series are intended to be discussion documents for teachers who are concerned with specialized interests of the profession.

Library of Congress Cataloging in Publication Data

Tchudi, Stephen N., 1924-
    Teaching writing in the content areas: elementary
school.

    Bibliography: p.
    1. English language—Composition and exercises.
2. Education—Curricula. I. Tchudi, Susan J.
II. National Education Association of the United
States. III. Title.
LB1576.T36   1983   372.6'23   82-22353
ISBN 0-8106-3226-8

CONTENTS

The Authors

Stephen N. Tchudi is Professor of English at Michigan State University, East Lansing.

Susan J. Tchudi is Associate Professor of English at Central Michigan University, Mt. Pleasant.

The Advisory Panel

Edna Mae Cahoon, first grade teacher, Malta Elementary School, Malta, Idaho

Michael E. Crane, Head Teacher, Pomona School, Pomona, New Jersey

Joyce J. Dahlquist, classroom teacher, Western Primary School, and adjunct faculty, Indiana University at Kokomo

Karla F. C. Holloway, Assistant Professor of English, Western Michigan University, Kalamazoo

James D. Phillips, Learning Disabilities Resource Room Teacher, and Chairman, Special Education Department, Yates Elementary School, Lexington, Kentucky

Kevin J. Swick, Professor of Education, University of South Carolina, Columbia

Richard A. Woolway, classroom teacher, Noble School, Bakersfield, California

Introduction

WRITING IN THE CONTENT AREAS— WHAT IS IT? WHY DO IT?

These days no one seems satisfied with the way Johnny and Jane write: not parents, not school administrators, not the media, not teachers, not even Johnny and Jane themselves. There are no cure-alls for this "literacy crisis," but one of the most exciting ways for teachers to help their students become more effective writers is through writing in the content areas: using language as the medium through which subject-matter learning takes place.

Of course, all writing has content. One can no more write without content than make an omelet without eggs. This publication suggests, however, that teachers be concerned not only with the language children use to express academic content, but with the accuracy of the content as well; that writing skills be sharpened on subject-matter projects, not just on isolated language arts exercises.

The relationship between language and content is not a recent discovery. The Greeks, insisting that the rhetorician be knowledge-able in many fields, saw the good public orator as one who could skillfully and persuasively marshal arguments on a wide range of subjects. During the Middle Ages, interest in content and language was revived; the language subjects of *grammar*, *rhetoric*, and *dialectic* (or logic) in the medieval curriculum were said to underlie such content-area disciplines as mathematics and natural science. In our own time another revival of interest in content-area writing is occurring. English/language arts specialists have observed that writing skills taught in isolation from content are not likely to be learned successfully. Students need to apply their language skills to real communications tasks, including writing in science, geography, social studies, mathematics, and vocational and career education.

Writing can also offer a teacher ways of eliciting information that are far more interesting to students (and teacher) than conventional examinations. For example, when studying the Amazon River Basin, the teacher who has students write vividly about an imaginary journey up the Amazon will help them understand the river in ways missed by the teacher who merely has them fill in blanks on an answer sheet. Similarly, when students write imaginatively about scientific principles—say, using their knowledge from a unit on fuels to write a futuristic story about transportation—they will learn their subject more effectively than when they merely master the basic

5

concepts in the textbook.

Writing is a practical skill, one of the most useful a student can learn, but it is valuable for more than classnotes, examinations, and research reports. Writing in the content areas can transform notetaking—the writing down of facts to be remembered—into journal keeping, when students interact with and respond to subject matter content. It can turn the traditional unit on the business letter into a real exercise in communication when students write genuine letters to live people in an attempt to learn something for class. It can change examination writing from regurgitation to imaginative synthesis and integration of ideas.

The claims of writing in the content areas to be part of the curriculum are many, but those that follow articulate some of the most persuasive reasons for all teachers to attend to the teaching of writing as well as to the teaching of content or subject matter.

1. *Writing about a subject helps students learn better*. The outcome of content writing programs is not simply improved language skills (an important end in itself), but improved learning of subject matter. If writing provides opportunities for students to play with ideas and concepts, then students will come to understand the subject more richly and deeply than before.

2. *Writing about content has practical payoff*. Perhaps the biggest reason Johnny and Jane do not write well is that they have not had enough practice doing it. Teachers whose students write frequently on content-area topics are providing a great service to those students, including short-term payoff (better writing of school papers) and long-range rewards (becoming successful writers at higher levels of education and in the real world).

3. *Content writing often motivates reluctant writers*. English compositions are often badly written because the topics are bland and banal: "My Summer Vacation," "The Most Unforgettable Character I Ever Met." Many so-called nonwriters are merely writers waiting for an engaging content-area topic to come along: *computers, science, history, futurism*. Writing about content gives substance to student writing and helps inspire many inexperienced and previously unmotivated writers.

4. *Content writing develops all language skills*. Although the principal concern here is writing, language skills are so tightly interwoven that a better title for this publication might be *Teaching* Literacy *in the Content Areas: Reading, Writing, Listening, Speaking*. The model units demonstrate this by including supplementary reading, questions for talk and discussion, and even opportunities for drama and media composition.

5. *Teaching writing teaches thinking.* According to an old, but accurate, cliche', one does not understand an idea fully until one can write about it. We do not believe that one can teach thinking the same way one can teach the multiplication tables, but it is clear that a student who is a good writer is generally perceived by his or her teachers as an effective thinker as well. Learning to write involves learning to think, and writing is unique in allowing students not only to think, but to display the products of their thinking in a form that invites further contemplation.

HOW TO USE THIS BOOK

This book is written with a very broad audience in mind. It is designed both for teachers who have previously taught writing but who want to move into content-writing topics and for teachers who are novices at teaching writing but who think it might be important to do with their students.

Part I, then, offers a primer for the writing teacher—novice or experienced—some basic principles and procedures that show all teachers just how easy it is to start content writing in their classes. Part II offers specific examples—model units and lessons—and some teachers may wish to turn directly to that section and examine the pedagogical principles later. Part III, concerned with applications and extensions, shows teachers how to move beyond the sample lessons to develop specific materials for their own classrooms.

Throughout the book, we have taken pains to show that teaching writing in the content areas is *not* an add-on, not just another burden for the busy teacher. Content writing can be integrated within the existing day, within the existing curriculum, enhancing instruction rather than becoming an independent component of it. Even theme evaluation, which is often perceived as a task so large as to discourage teachers from teaching writing, can be integrated naturally into the content teaching of a class.

This book also has another broad audience in mind, an indirect audience: the students of the teachers who will read it. We have taught writing in the content areas in inner-city schools, in a summer writing camp for youngsters from disadvantaged settings, in suburban schools, in afterschool young writers' workshops, and even to college students and faculty members. We have seen that it can energize previously uninspired writers—of whom there are a vast number in this country. Finally, then, we hope that the ideas and examples presented here will motivate the teachers who read them to join the ranks of those teachers who already see the enormous value and pleasure involved in teaching writing in the content areas.

Part I

A Primer on Teaching Writing in the Content Areas

You don't need a college degree in English to teach content-area writing. You don't have to be an expert in grammar or know how to diagram a sentence or be able to explain the difference between a direct and indirect object. You don't have to be a walking dictionary or thesaurus, and you don't have to be an expert on contemporary usage and style. You don't even need to feel you are an outstanding writer yourself (although that certainly wouldn't hurt). In short, you don't have to be trained as a specialist to teach interdisciplinary writing.

As a matter of fact, if you are *not* a specialist, you may have a distinct advantage: namely, that you don't have a preconceived notion about how writing "must" be taught. Too often the teaching of writing has been made overly complex by specialists, especially in teaching students complicated and abstract concepts of rhetoric and grammar. This primer keeps things simple, not because we underestimate your intelligence or experience, but because you can carry out content-area writing instruction successfully if you keep in mind just a few precepts and apply them consistently. As a matter of fact, one principle is central to our philosophy of content-area writing. From it, all else follows:

Keep content at the center of the writing process.

This principle gives *clarity of content* top priority. Students first need to know a subject well and then must be committed to presenting their thoughts clearly to an audience. Good writing follows from that formula. You probably know from your own experience the effect knowing the material can have on your writing. Can you recall going into an exam feeling shaky about your mastery of the subject? What happened to your writing? Did it become weak, tentative, evasive, or uncertain, betraying your limited grasp of the content? Was it different when you went to the exam with the material clearly in mind? Chances are it was then more confident, firm, and vigorous, even forceful and clear.

But good writing involves more than mere subject matter knowledge. Many adults know volumes but cannot write successfully. Sometimes that can be traced to a failure to focus knowledge, to take a stance or point of view toward it, or to phrase the material for a particular kind of reader. Too many school writing assignments use writing solely as a way to "prove" mastery of content by repeating what was learned in class and from texts. In such cases, students do not focus their writing or take a stand on the material. In contrast, a well-designed writing activity builds in stance and point of view and even provides an audience for writing to assist students in organizing their knowledge and in selecting a structure for it in writing.

Much of teaching writing in the content areas consists not in telling students *how* to write, but in creating situations where they want to write and want to write well, using their subject-matter knowlege in the process. The four steps discussed in the next few pages are those used in our own teaching and in developing the model content-area activities that appear in Part II.

A PROCEDURE FOR DEVELOPING CONTENT-AREA WRITING LESSONS

1. Determine content objectives. Whatever you are teaching, the first question to answer is: What do you want your students to learn? Content-area writing works best when it involves *discovery, synthesis,* and *inquiry* rather than recitation of factual material. Although teachers *can* use writing to have students merely list what they know on a subject, often a multiple-choice or short-answer test is more efficient and truer to the use of language for that purpose. Save the real writing assignments for the times when you want students to put their learning together and apply it to new situations.

As an illustration, suppose a teacher was doing a unit on the solar system. In a factually oriented class, the learning objectives might focus on such matters as knowing the names of the planets, their location in space relative to the sun, their characteristics, and, perhaps, the origins of their names in classical mythology. Such information—if it were the only aim of the unit—would be examined most easily through multiple-choice or short-answer tests.

A teacher interested in having students *synthesize* and *apply* their knowledge might have a broader set of objectives, such as helping students come to—

- Understand (or at least partially comprehend) the vastness of the solar system—to feel the distances, not just know them.
- Explore the possibilities for travel to the other planets (possibly as an antidote to the impressions created by popular television programs).
- Understand the various theories of the origins of our solar system and weigh the evidence supporting each theory.

Unit objectives would be rather broad, possibly creating the framework for several weeks' work. Presumably the teacher would also create more specific objectives for individual class lessons and/or writing activities.

In any event, the cardinal principle is that *content objectives should be established first*, prior to the writing activities.

2. Develop writing ideas to explore the objectives. Often teachers think of writing assignments in only two discourse modes— the essay and the report—and give them in barebones fashion, with few instructions to the writer:

> Write an essay or report on the origins of the solar system
> and explain the locations of the nine planets.

Sometimes the assignment specifies length as well:

> Your paper should be at least two pages (or ten pages or
> 500 words or 1,000 words in length).

Most of us have probably written papers on topics that were not spelled out in much more detail. Such assignments often fail because they do not explore the range of writing forms available to the student and they supply little assistance to the writer. By their very brevity they invite failure.

There are a number of ways to express content ideas in writing, and a good interdisciplinary writing program will explore many of them. The principal objectives of the solar system unit, for example, can be explored in several different modes of discourse, including the following:

> *Fiction*—"Write a short story about travel from one
> planet to another, with your hero or heroine telling about
> what he/she observes."

10

Journalism—"You are the editor of *Interplanetary Gazette*, a video newspaper that is circulated throughout the solar system. Write some news stories telling what life is like on each planet."

Media—"Suppose you were preparing a television special about the solar system. Write a plan for the program. What kinds of information and film shots would you want to include?"

The writing can, of course, be done in more conventional forms of school writing:

Essay—"What do you think about the possibilities for space travel in your lifetime? Write an essay in which you suggest just how common you think interplanetary travel will be by, say, the year 2050."

Report—"Rocketry has come a long way since World War II, when crude rockets were first used in warfare. Make a study of the major advancements in rocket design in the past forty years and write a report."

Figure 1 is a list of the different kinds of discourse forms that can easily be drawn upon for content-area assignments. In our own teaching we use this list and try to create a range of choices for students so that they are regularly encountering new ways to express their knowledge. The essential question for the teacher at this point is: How can students best get their ideas on the subject into writing? Sometimes the form of a *play* or a *story* will be best. At others, a letter written to another person may be a good option. Older students may find expository writing easier to do than some of the so-called creative writing forms, but creative writing of poems, plays, stories, songs is an appropriate way to express ideas at all levels.

Whenever possible, we offer our students a range of writing ideas with several different ways to satisfy the main assignment. We have already given five options on the solar system topic. But teachers can have students consider projects that go beyond spoken or written language into art and music:

Draw or paint your impressions of the planet Venus.

Or:

Find some classical music that fits your impressions of the planet Venus and play it for the class or to back up your drawing of what you think the planet looks like.

11

SOME DISCOURSE FORMS FOR CONTENT WRITING

Journals and diaries
  (real or imaginary)
Biographical sketches
Anecdotes and stories:
  from experience
  as told by others
Thumbnail sketches:
  of famous people
  of places
  of content ideas
  of historical events
Guess who/what descriptions
Letters:
  personal reactions
  observations
  public/informational
  persuasive:
    to the editor
    to public officials
    to imaginary people
    from imaginary places
Requests
Applications
Memos
Resume's and summaries
Poems
Plays
Stories
Fantasy
Adventure
Science fiction
Historical stories
Dialogues and conversations
Children's books
Telegrams
Editorials
Commentaries
Responses and rebuttals
Newspaper "fillers"
Fact books or fact sheets
School newspaper stories
Stories or essays for local papers
Proposals
Case studies:
  school problems
  local issues
  national concerns
  historical problems
  scientific issues
Songs and ballads
Demonstrations
Poster displays

Reviews:
  books (including textbooks)
  films
  outside reading
  television programs
  documentaries
Historical "you are there" scenes
Scence notes:
  observations
  science notebook
  reading reports
  lab reports
Math:
  story problems
  solutions to problems
  record books
  notes and observations
Responses to literature
Utopian proposals
Practical proposals
Interviews:
  actual
  imaginary
Directions:
  how-to
  school or neighborhood guide
  survival manual
Dictionaries and lexicons
Technical reports
Future options, notes on:
  careers, employment
  school and training
  military/public service
Written debates
Taking a stand:
  school issues
  family problems
  state or national issues
  moral questions
Books and booklets
Informational monographs
Radio scripts
TV scenarios and scripts
Dramatic scripts
Notes for improvised drama
Cartoons and cartoon strips
Slide show scripts
Puzzles and word searches
Prophecy and predictions
Photos and captions
Collage, montage, mobile,
  sculpture

FIGURE 1

12

While these latter projects are not the heart of a *writing* program, they suggest yet another interdisciplinary connection and use some of the essential processes of writing, including finding an idea, locating information, organizing the information for an audience, and presenting it.

Finally, we like to give our students one additional choice:

> If none of the ideas I've given you about writing about the solar system appeals to you, make up your own idea. Just check with me before you begin to write.

The more students write, the more likely they are to have developed their imaginations and the more likely they are to choose that open-ended topic, in essence, inventing their own assignments. So much the better, we think.

As part of our writing projects, we also try to build in an audience for student writers. Including provisions for an audience in an assignment helps students write for someone other than the teacher and adds a strong element of reality to the writing process. The audience for writing can be an imaginary one—especially for younger writers:

> After months of travel through outer space, you have landed your craft on Mars. Once you have stretched your legs and gotten use to the lower gravity, you decide to send a Space-O-Gram back to your earthbound family. What do you tell them about what you have seen?

Sometimes the audience becomes the other students, who can be invited to join in the fantasy and role play the audience or even write back from the point of view of that audience:

> Your parent has just sent you a Space-O-Gram from Mars describing life on that planet. What additional questions do you have? Write a Space-O-Gram back requesting more information.

Often, however, the audiences for student writing can be real, giving writers a sense that their writing can be helpful in the real world:

> Write to the National Aeronautics and Space Administration in Washington, D.C., requesting information on NASA's future plans for interplanetary space travel.

13

Other audiences for student writing can range from the class to other students in the school to administrators to parents to public officials (at the state or local level) to nationally famous people. Whenever feasible, then, add focus to writing activities by specifying the real or imaginary audience for them.

A good composition assignment or activity not only needs to be explicit, it should also make clear to students precisely what they must do to complete the assignment successfully. For example, inexperienced writers almost invariably want to know something about length—"How long does it have to be?"—a habit often learned in classes where teachers had them write to specific word lengths—500 or 1,000. Instead of turning students into word counters, help them understand how long a composition should be in terms of its intrinsic need to satisfy the assignment. The appropriate length of a piece of writing is *long enough to get the job done*, but teachers can supply some hints:

> Write up an interview between the astronaut who has just returned from the moon and a reporter for the evening news. Think of five or six good questions for the interviewer to ask and then write the astronaut's answers.

Or:

> Have your astronaut write a summary of his/her observations about the possibility of life on planet Mars for the Director of NASA. The Director is a busy person, so make the summary as concise as possible, but don't leave out any important details.

The assignments should also make clear the purpose of the writing (especially if students are writing an examination). Students should know from the teacher's oral or written comments just why this writing is being done:

> To show that you understand how our solar system works, write as if you were a comet, just entering the system and heading toward the sun, describing what you see.

It is also important for the oral or written assignment to include some guidance to get students started finding any material they need to complete it successfully. This might be as simple as reading a chapter in the textbook:

> After you have read the chapter on planets in your text,

14

pick one planet and write a brief description of it in your journal.

More often (and more imaginatively) the assignment can suggest sources of ideas beyond the classroom:

The Astronomers' Club invites guests to its meetings. If you think you'd like to attend one, let me know and we'll make arrangements. That way you'll have some firsthand information for use in your solar system paper.

Or:

Go to the library and get a biography of Galileo. After you've read it, either write a description of the solar system as he imagined it, or pretend you are Galileo and write a letter to a friend describing all the difficulties you are having persuading people to accept your view of the solar system.

No single written assignment can fully teach writing or prepare students to engage with complete success in the writing process. But we hope this section has helped teachers see the range of content-area writing possibilities that exists, as well as the importance of careful design and **planning** of the assignment for a successful student writing experience.

3. Teach writing and learning. Once the assignment is made, the real content teaching begins, but as we emphasized earlier, *teaching content is also teaching writing.* This can be divided into several stages: *prewriting, writing, revising, copyediting,* and *presenting and publishing.*

Prewriting. Before students put pen to paper, their preparation is very important. This is the time when they either master their basic content or fail to understand it, with predictable results in their writing. Although teachers at the upper levels may want to assign an impromptu theme from time to time as preparation for examination writing, the impromptu, with its focus on instant writing, is generally a poor form for practice; it is something only advanced writers can do successfully. We urge teachers to spend a great deal of time at the prewriting/learning stage—an hour, a day, sometimes a week or more—helping students gather information and prepare to write. Good content teaching enters at this point as students read, discuss, and think about their material.

15

Here are some ways the teacher can focus the prewriting stage:

■ Have students keep logs or notebooks or journals of their learning. These should contain basic notes or ideas, of course, but more important, they should provide students with an avenue to respond in personal terms to what they are learning. They can write about their puzzlements, amazements, astounding and interesting facts, and things "I never knew before." Journals of this sort are usually left ungraded, simply checked from time to time by the teacher for their informational content.

■ Provide prewriting discussions of the topic and assignment. Sometimes this can be done in small groups; at others, through teacher-led discussion. In the discussion students can talk over questions about the assignment, where they can find information, the audience for the writing, the range of choices and options available.

■ Encourage students to develop their own set of planning strategies. *Don't require formal outlines for papers.* Instead, urge students to make plans, in writing, according to a pattern that feels comfortable to them. Some people like to make long, elaborate sets of notes before writing, others prefer to jot down just a few words. Still others like to go through their notebooks or journals, circling the important ideas and numbering them in order, finally jotting down a plan for writing as a final journal entry. Every writer needs to do some planning before writing, but the conventional outline inhibits more student writers than it helps.

Such written planning, even if done on scratch paper, helps the teacher ensure that the student has, in fact, mastered or understood the content material. If students cannot plan, jot down some notes or ideas on paper, the teacher has a clue that more prewriting is necessary.

■ Have students talk through their papers with the teacher or another student before writing. This oral strategy is extremely helpful in clarifying the thoughts and ideas of young writers before they commit themselves to writing. It need not take long—perhaps five or ten minutes—and it invariably produces good results in terms of the clarity and focus of the writing.

Writing. Many teachers think of the writing stage as a time to sit back and relax, a time to wait before the onslaught of another batch of papers for grading. But *as* students write, teachers can do much to help raise the quality of their writing and learning.

When students are writing during class time, the teacher can take an active role. For example, monitor facial expressions—they often tell when a student is starting to get in a jam and needs help. Float about the class during a writing assignment, glancing at first para-

16

graphs and rough beginnings, offering advice if it seems needed and respecting students' need to be left alone if your presence makes them nervous. In other words, help students get it right *while* they are writing and encourage them to solve their problems the first time around. This helps cut down on the amount of revision needed later.

Also encourage students to talk to one another during the writing process—unless, of course, the writing is an examination of some sort. There are great benefits from such forms of peer collaboration as encouraging writers to bounce ideas off one another, reading draft paragraphs aloud to seek advice, pumping their friends for new ideas. As long as this collaboration occurs publicly and within the spirit of fair play, there is no danger of students cheating or turning in something that is not their own.

Other ideas for teaching during the writing process:

■ Tell students not to worry about spelling, punctuation, and mechanics at the rough draft stage. If their concerns about correctness inhibit them from writing, however, encourage them to ask questions about correctness as items or problems come up. Be sure not to attach any penalties or embarrassment to such requests for help.

■ Provide assistance for students who get stuck with a writing block. Nine times out of ten such a block comes from a content failure: the writer just does not know what to say about the topic. But other problems can lead writers to freeze while writing. If students cannot get the opening paragraph down on paper, suggest that they write the second paragraph first and not worry about the beginning until later. Sometimes a little free association will help unclog a pen. Some writers even write the *end* of their papers before going back to write the earlier parts. Conversation is also an unblocker, and the teacher can help out by simply saying, "Tell me what it is you want to write about." Once the student has told about his or her plan, the teacher can say, "You've just done it. Now all you have to do is write it down."

■ Provide as much support as possible through the content matter of the writing. Help students focus on what they know and the audience with whom they will be sharing their knowledge. That kind of focus will bring clarity to their writing.

■ Create the tone of a collaborative workshop in the class. Don't let the room be a silent tomb where everyone works at writing in isolation.

It is probably obvious that we generally favor in-class to out-of-class writing. When students are writing on school time, teachers can control the process much more successfully. However, even if students write at home, teachers can monitor their progress. For example, teachers can urge students to keep in touch as they write and to give them daily progress reports on papers being written outside class. If a student has some writing problems and cannot solve them, it is better to hear about them before the day the paper is due.

Revising. Research in writing shows that astonishingly few young writers—elementary, secondary, even college level—know much about revising a paper. To many students, "revise" simply means, "Make a clean copy in your best handwriting." However, as numerous professional writers have reported, good writing usually means good *re*writing. Drafts are often rough and inaccurate, representing a struggle to get words down on the page. Rewriting brings focus and clarity. It is important that teachers encourage revision as a part of every paper they assign.

It is also important to distinguish between *revising* and *copyediting.* The latter has to do with the surface correctness of the manuscript, and it should occur at the end of the writing process. *Revising* means working with the content of a paper—moving ideas around, adding needed information, taking out redundant material.

Revising can often be a community activity, with students serving successfully as their own editors, commenting on their papers and making suggestions for changes. To initiate a group revision session, divide the class into threes or fours or fives, either self-selected or teacher-assigned groups. Then have students share papers—sometimes with the author reading the draft of his/her paper aloud to the group, sometimes with papers passed around for written comments and responses. Caution students that this is not a red-penciling session for nitpicking about spelling and grammar. Nor is it an opportunity for cutting down their neighbors. Rather, it is a way for writers to get some sense of how their papers affect a small group of readers. It is the single best way we know of to help writers see the kinds of changes they need to make.

Small group revising of papers also helps solve a problem that may be the biggest barrier to teachers' doing more content-area writing: the theme-correcting burden. Many teachers we have met say they would like to do more writing in their classes, but they do not have time to correct all the papers students produce. To such teachers we recommend peer revising. It reduces theme grading to a reasonable level in several ways:

1. It places the responsibility for revision with the proper person—the *writer.*
2. The group work involved creates flexible time for the teacher to use for individual conferences, providing concrete help on a

face-to-face basis that is far more efficient than writing comments on themes.

3. The papers turned in are better than those that are simply dashed off in class and given to the teacher to read. Many teachers who use group revision report theme reading to be a pleasure, not a chore, consisting primarily of logging in good, successful papers rather than penning critical comments on a batch of rough drafts.

Of course, the teacher cannot be passive in peer revising sessions—they are not successful by magic. The teacher needs to structure them carefully so that students know what is expected and precisely how to go about revising one another's work. To begin such a session, review the assignment with the class, reminding students what was expected, for whom the paper was written, the kind of content it was to contain, and so on. Then have students respond to the paper in terms of the content that it presents. Is it clear? Does it make sense? Can other students understand it? Could outsiders understand it? What changes would help? A good way to organize these sessions is to provide the class with a sheet with a few focus questions for the day as shown in Figure 2. A longer list of questions for teachers to use to make their own revising sheets appears in Figure 3. Naturally, the complexity of these question can be adjusted to match the skills of students.

SAMPLE REVISING SHEET

Today I want you to focus on whether or not the writer kept the audience in mind during the writing process. Answer these questions in your small groups.

1. Who is the best audience for this paper as it is written? Can you describe the people who would be most interested in it?

2. Did the writer tell the audience everything it needs to know to understand the topic? Help the writer figure out if anything is left out.

3. Did the writer perhaps tell too much? Is there more information here than an audience can possibly handle? Help the writer figure out where to cut.

4. After you have completed your small group discussion, write a note to the author, reacting to the paper as if you were a member of the audience.

FIGURE 2

19

OTHER QUESTIONS FOR REVISING GROUPS

Note: Do not have students ask *all* these questions (or similar ones) at every revising session. Rather, pick some questions that seem most appropriate to your assignment and have the students work on two or three each time.

PURPOSE

- Where is this writing headed? Can readers clearly tell?
- Is it on one track, or does it shoot off in new directions?
- Is the writer trying to do too much? Too little?
- Does the author seem to *care* about his her/writing?

CONTENT

- When you're through, can you easily summarize this piece or retell it in your own words?
- Can a reader understand it easily?
- Are there parts that you found confusing?
- Are there parts that need more explanation or evidence?
- Are there places where the writer said too much, or overexplained the subject?
- Can the reader visualize the subject?
- Does it hold your interest all the way through?
- Did you learn something new from this paper?

ORGANIZATION

- Do the main points seem to be in the right order?
- Does the writer give you enough information so that you know what he/she is trying to accomplish?
- Does the writing begin smoothly? Does the writer take too long to get started?
- What about the ending? Does it end crisply and excitingly?

AUDIENCE

- Who are the readers for this writing? Does the writer seem to have them clearly in mind? Will they understand him/her?
- Does the writer assume too much from the audience? Too little?
- What changes does the writer need to make to better communicate with the audience?

LANGUAGE AND STYLE

- Is the paper interesting and readable? Does it get stuffy or dull?
- Can you hear the writer's voice and personality in it?
- Are all difficult words explained or defined?
- Does the writer use natural, lively language throughout?
- Are the grammar, spelling, and punctuation OK?

FIGURE 3

Not all teachers are comfortable with peer revision of papers. There can be some problems: students do not always give one another good advice; sometimes group members do not have rapport; and sometimes students give each other bland approval instead of needed criticism. Nevertheless, we strongly urge teachers to try peer revising more than once—don't just try it once and give it up if it doesn't seem to work right away. This method helps students learn to become responsible for the quality of their own work, and in that respect, it is one of the most important skills a young writer can master.

Copyediting. It is extremely important that teachers not introduce concerns for spelling, punctuation, and mechanics too early in the writing process. And it is important that students learn how to get their final copies into standard edited English. But such concerns should not take priority over matters of content.

Now is the time for teacher and students to be concerned with correctness, after the paper has been planned and organized and shaped and drafted and revised. Now is the time for the teacher to have students work on spelling problems and usage errors, guiding them to the correct forms. We believe it is crucial for the teacher to train students to take responsibility for the final correctness of their work. The teacher should not be a copyeditor.

A great deal has been written in recent years about the appropriateness of compelling all students, especially those who are members of racial and ethnic minorities, to write in a uniform standard English. In general, composition researchers have come to feel that it is inappropriate to try to eradicate the dialect of a student's upbringing, and, further, that dwelling on matters of correctness seldom teaches "good English" and often inhibits students from writing well. At the same time, there is a "real world," a world that penalizes and even ridicules those who do not adhere to the conventions of standard written English.

We suggest that the concern for correctness be introduced very gradually, and that at no time a student be made to feel that the dialect he or she uses quite comfortably at home and with peers is somehow inadequate or second-rate. Most dialects, in fact, are both sophisticated and appropriate for the situations in which they are used. The best route to correctness is through publishing student writing, a topic to be discussed next. Further, small group work is again helpful in giving students an awareness that the conventions of standard written English are not just arbitrary—they help people communicate more successfully. In a group of four or five students,

21

most major misspellings and usage errors can be identified, even with very young writers. The copyediting sessions will not always produce perfect papers, but they will help students learn how to go about this final stage of the process. We are confident that teachers who try group copyediting for a semester or a year will be happy with the results, and will see students grow in their ability to check their own papers.

However, teachers who are not satisfied with the results of these sessions can follow up with written comments and suggestions on the papers. We do *not* recommend marking every error on every paper, a chore that is time-consuming for the teacher and disheartening for the student. Rather, we suggest picking one or two errors that seem to come up regularly in the student's work and concentrating on those.

Above all, don't give student writers the impression that correctness is the be-all and end-all of writing. Keep the focus and the praise on *content*, and work on mechanics gradually, as a peripheral matter.

Presenting and publishing. Writing that is done solely for the teacher, or solely for a grade, is often not highly motivated. To motivate students to do their best writing, include provision for presentation and publication whenever possible. This can be as simple as posting papers on a bulletin board or having them read aloud to the class; or publishing class newspapers and magazines, using ditto or mimeograph to produce something students can take home and share. Pat Edwards, a teacher in New South Wales, Australia, has compiled a list of 101 different ways to publish student writing,[5] including the following:

- Books (individual books, collaborative books, textbooks written for the whole class)
- Newspapers (school news, family news, natural science reports)
- Magazines (on almost any conceivable subject matter topic)
- Plays (as a way of presenting written ideas for an audience)
- Letters (sent within the class through a postal system or letters actually mailed)
- Bulletin boards and display centers
- School assemblies (for presenting work orally, often with audiovisual aids)
- Storefront displays (getting student writing out into the community)
- Tape recording (to create an oral library of writing).

22

Publishing writing provides an incentive for students to do a good job of revising and copyediting, but more significantly, it shows them that writing is important because it brings them a readership and a response or reaction. It is the payoff to the writing process.

4. Followup. Too often writing assignments seem to be made in isolation, as one-time-only events unrelated to the rest of the class and its activities. When writing in the content areas is well taught, it provides natural possibilities for additional work. One writing idea leads to another: a piece of fantasy writing becomes the starting point for a series of stories; a kitchen science experiment with electricity suggests ideas for a booklet on similar experiments. Other areas of a topic can be explored through writing, leading to a classroom where students have a piece of content writing in the works at all times. Even the presentation stage of writing can lead to followup activities, as one piece of student writing generates a response from students that encourages them to start off on a new writing project. Writing leads to writing, as the model lessons that follow demonstrate.

LESSON FORM FOR CONTENT-AREA WRITING ACTIVITIES

1. Determine content objectives.

2. Develop writing ideas that explore the content concepts.

3. Teach writing and learning:
   A. Prewriting
   B. Writing
   C. Revising
   D. Copyediting
   E. Presenting and Publishing

4. Followup

FIGURE 4

Part II

Model Units for Teaching Writing in the Content Areas

Teachers can study the units that follow in one of two ways: (1) they can read them and glean the principles of interdisciplinary teaching from them before designing their own lessons, or (2) they can test some of the lessons in their own classes. We think the second option is preferable in that teaching, like writing, is a learn-by-doing skill. The comments and suggestions will probably make more sense if the ideas are tested in the classroom. In this case, it will be helpful to know that each unit is designed to stand independently of others, and none requires any previous experience teaching writing in the content areas.

The units vary in length. Some can be completed in a day or two; others may require a week. Drawing on the suggested followup activities, some can be extended to a month or a year. Teachers should not feel it is necessary to make their content lessons as complete and lengthy as the ones described here—they can whittle them down to the size that fits their own class. Further, these are lesson ideas, not blueprints. Many alternative ideas and teaching strategies have been included so that units can be adapted to the needs of students.

FAMILIES

Families is a topic that students at almost any grade level can profitably study. To demonstrate how writing in the content areas can work for the youngest students in the school, we have designed this unit for first and second graders. It shows that even students who have just mastered the rudiments of writing can use composition as a way of learning more about themselves and others. The first part of the lesson uses personal writing to explore feelings about the family; the second part focuses on science and family resemblance; the followup activity shows a way to extend this unit into social studies.

Content Objectives

■ To heighten children's understanding of the roles and relationships among members of their own families.
■ To help children understand how their families are similar to and different from other families.
■ To help children discover how individuals within a family are alike and different.
■ To explore how families in other cultures live compared to the child's own family.

Writing and Learning

Part 1. Personal Writing

As part of exploring family roles and relationships, students will write about a family experience—a typical incident or a special event—that involved their whole family.

Prewriting

Begin this unit by sharing books that show different kinds of family structures and family relationships. Some good ones include the following:

Jan Slepian, *Lester's Turn* (New York: Macmillan, 1981)
Paul Zindel, *I Love My Mother* (New York: Harper and
Row, 1975)

Charlotte Zolotow, *A Father Like That* (New York: Harper and Row, 1971)
Norma Klein, *Confessions of an Only Child* (New York: Pantheon, 1974).

After reading several books aloud—possibly over a several-day period—have the children talk about their own families. Some students may be only children; some may come from large families; some may live in single parent homes; some may be from foster or adoptive homes; some may live in reconstituted families with step-parents; some may live with grandparents. Of course, in any discussion of family lifestyles, it is important that teachers be both sensitive and nonjudgmental. Their role at this point is to allow children to discuss their family relationships and their feelings about these relationships. The children need tell no deep secrets; nor need they say anything that might embarrass themselves. Most first and second graders have many good and interesting things to say about their family life.

After teacher and children have read and talked, have children draw a picture of their family and then share it with a friend. Encourage them to describe the picture telling who each family member is and something about each one. Then have them write a sentence or two at the bottom of the picture telling something they like about their family.

Next have a discussion with the children about activities, experiences, or special events they have shared with their family. Emphasize both special occasions and events that might not even seem significant to them: birthday parties, holiday celebrations, Friday night dinners at a favorite restaurant, sharing responsibility for a pet, sharing household chores, summer cookouts, summer vacations, sharing sports interests, visiting grandparents. Then have students choose one event they would like to write about.

Writing

If the children are early-in-the-year first graders, they may not yet be writing independently. In that case, you may take dictation from them. If you are working alone, the process may continue for several days. During seatwork, children can come to your desk one by one to dictate their stories. Be sure to take down their exact words, to maintain the integrity of the story and to aid them in reading what they have written. If you have parent volunteers or upper-grade children to help you, the dictation process can be completed in a shorter period of time.

Older first graders and second graders will be able to write independently—although a few may still need to dictate to the teacher. While the children are writing, walk around the room asking questions of those who seem to be stuck or who are writing very generally, without specifics. Begin teaching the concept of "showing" rather than "telling" and ask questions to help them make their writing detailed.

During the writing process, one concern of many students is how to spell the words they want to use. Good teachers of writing handle the teaching of spelling in different ways. Some simply spell the word for the child; others write all the words that children want spelled on the board, giving everyone an opportunity to see the words others are using. Either way, children will not be sidetracked in their thinking about what they want to say. It is important *not* to send them to dictionaries at this point in the writing process. Their goal is to get their ideas on paper. Later they will make corrections that make the paper readable for others.

Revising and Sharing

After they have written about their experience, have the children again share their work with a friend, who may ask questions that suggest new ideas to add to the story. Teachers may want to read aloud the stories of the early first graders, gathering responses from the whole class. However, even the newest writers can often do a good job of reading a story someone else has taken down in dictation.

Encourage the writers to jot down ideas for additional writing in the margins of their papers or above the lines on which they have written. Children are sometimes hesitant to mess up a paper that has required so much effort, but tell them they will be making a final copy so that they can make their writing look just as they wish. From the earliest grades it is important to give students the idea that revising is a natural part of the writing process. During the sharing of stories and noting of ideas, circulate around the room, complimenting children and asking questions that may encourage them to write more. This is also a good time to instruct in mechanics and spelling, showing individuals what corrections need to be made and why.

Then, before any rewriting, have students hand in their drafts. At this point teachers can make any necessary final corrections before distributing the corrected papers to children for rewriting.

After the recopying, create a bulletin board display, using these stories with the family pictures drawn earlier. This display is an excellent exhibit for parents' night or a PTA meeting.

Part 2. Science Writing

After studying how families resemble one another physically, students now write a description of the likenesses they see among their own family members. These writings are then placed in a class book.

Prewriting

To begin the unit, read students a children's book that describes family resemblances and inherited traits such as *Your Family Tree* by Jean Kamaiko and Kate Rosenthal. Discuss how members of a family may resemble one another, and ask questions about resemblances in the students' own families.

> Do members of your family have the same color hair? eyes? Do they have similar builds or body shapes? short? tall? thin? stocky? Do members of your family have straight or curly hair? Do they have similar features like noses? chins? teeth? Do people ever tell you that you look like someone else in your family? Which ones? Which members of your family most resemble one another?

Tell youngsters to *observe* members of their family at home and look for more similar traits. Ask them to bring in family pictures, preferably color photographs. If this is not feasible, provide time in school for children to draw pictures of family members showing the common physical traits. Drawing skill is not of the essence here; nor is it a problem if red hair is shown with a flaming scarlet crayon.

Not all students will have complete biological families on which to base this informal research, and as noted previously, it is important not to put the child from a nontraditional family structure in an embarrassing position. Some children may therefore do this project for, say, their foster family or for brothers and sisters but not stepbrothers and stepsisters.

Allow several days for studying photographs and creating pictures. The children can make lists of resemblances something like these:

Curly Hair	*Crooked Baby Finger*
Mom	Dad
Jody	Me
Grandpa (once upon a time)	

Freckles	*Red Hair*
Mom	Grandma
Grandma	Me
Aunt Sarah	Daddy
David	
Me	

As in the earlier part of this lesson, the new first graders may need help with these lists, the teacher serving as scribe and helping children read the words written down.

Writing

After children have completed their prewriting lists and have accumulated photographs or drawings, have them decide what family traits they would like to write about in a book. They may use their lists to check off the traits that seem to be most striking in their family. When they have settled on three to five traits, help them start on the rough drafts, writing about a separate trait on each page. One page, for example, may discuss the curly-haired members of the family; another, what it is like to be a member of the tallest family in the school. While children are writing, circulate throughout the room asking questions and seeking elaboration, as well as helping students put their ideas on paper by dictation if necessary.

Revising

Exchange papers and have peer readers respond to the writing, asking questions and suggesting corrections. During this stage of the process, be available to answer questions about spelling and mechanics. As much as possible, show children how to make corrections right on the paper. Don't dwell on rules; simply show them the right way to do things.

Preparing Final Copy

When the papers have been revised, distribute nine-by-twelve-inch construction paper. Students can use one piece of construction paper for each trait they have written about, mounting their photographs or drawings at the top of the page and recopying their writing below with a fine felt-tip pen or a freshly sharpened crayon. When all the stories have been completed, laminate the pages, punch holes in them, and assemble them in a notebook to be available to the class.

Followup

The Families theme invites a number of spinoff oral and written composition activities:

■ Invite an elderly person to class to talk with the children about his or her family many years ago.

■ Have students write letters—other than thank-you notes—to relatives, initiating a flow of correspondence with other members of their family.

■ Bring in a cage full of gerbils and have students observe and write notes about gerbil family life.

■ Let students write about imaginary families, on this planet or elsewhere.

■ Bring in books on family life in other cultures and have children discuss and possibly write about how their family life differs from that of young people in other countries.

THE FOODS WE EAT

"You can't start too early to teach people to eat right." Most parents, nutritionists, and educators would agree with that statement. But this unit does more than simply attempt to teach students some basics of nutrition—it also involves them in understanding some aspects of the food chain and the source of our food. It is truly interdisciplinary in its use of mathematics and writing, two subjects not often linked in the schools.

Content Objectives

The students will:

■ Examine the ways in which foods help our bodies grow strong and remain healthy (nutrition).
■ Use a variety of measuring and computation skills in following recipes (mathematics).
■ Study the people and jobs involved in growing food and processing it for use in the home (social studies).

Writing Idea

After studying about and preparing some food, the children will make a class book. The first section will be a collaborative writing project with contributions from the whole class, describing the processes of growing and making food. The remainder of the book will consist of one page contributed by each child in which he/she describes some aspect of how food gets from the farm to the home.

Writing and Learning

Prewriting

Begin this unit by asking students to talk about what they know about food. What are your favorite foods? What do you know about foods that are good for you? What foods are considered junk foods? Where do the things you like to eat come from? What are the ingredients? Who puts the ingredients together? Where does the food we eat come from geographically?

After the discussion, begin with one or several of the following prewriting projects. Have students keep informal logs or notebooks jotting down their ideas and observations based on each activity.

Speaker. Invite an expert on nutrition to give an informal lecture and answer questions about the basic food groups and what our bodies receive from each of them. Next let students create simple charts (either a whole-class chart or pages in individual notebooks) describing what they eat for a period of time and where this fits into the basic food groups.

Make a Treat. Ask students to bring in a recipe for a favorite treat. Depending on the cooking facilities available in the school, create some of these treats—preferably those that are nutritious. Before preparing the food, instruct the children in basic measurement, using sand and water instead of flour and milk to learn how to measure a cup, half cup, quarter cup, tablespoon, teaspoon, and so forth. Then prepare the treats, allowing students to do as much of the measuring and mixing as possible. During the preparations, discuss where all the ingredients come from. Where does milk come from? eggs? What is flour made of? Why is some sugar white and some brown? What is shortening?

Research Teams. Split the class into groups to raise and answer questions about food and its processing. Yes, milk comes from a cow, but where do cows live? Who takes care of them? How does the milk get from the farm into the container?... What's in a soft drink? Where are soft drinks made? Are they good or bad for you?... What's in a pizza? How do you make one? Are pizzas good for you? Groups should jot down all their ideas on cards or sheets of paper, and individual group members may decide to find out answers to particular parts of a question or issue. In addition, the group research can draw on other resources the teacher arranges for the unit, including:

- *Books.* Ask the media center specialist or librarian to prepare a book cart on the topic for class use.
- *People.* Community members—parents, farmers, food industry workers, university or college extension service people—have expertise to share with children and feel honored to be invited to class.
- *Films.* Again check the media center for films to show the class.
- *Field Trips.* If at all possible, take students on trips—to a dairy farm (or farm within the city zoo), a chicken farm, a bottling plant. These places are usually happy to provide tours and may supply youngsters with some interesting free brochures as well.

Throughout this phase, encourage children to keep jotting down ideas in their logs or notebooks. They need not keep elaborate notes, but it is a good idea to help them cultivate the habit and realization that written recordkeeping is a good way to remember things.

Writing and Revising

Part I of the writing is a collaborative project. Tape a large piece of newsprint on the board and act as a scribe as the children compose. The subject is how food, in general, is grown and gets to the home—the food processing chain. Have children take turns describing the process while you write ideas on newsprint. When they have told you all they can remember, go back through the writing with them. Reread what they have written and ask if they want to make changes. Is there anything else to add? Is there anything they want to leave out? Are there repetitions? Do they want to arrange the information in different order? As the children make suggestions, serve as their scribe/editor and show them how to make changes on a manuscript. Draw lines through unnecessary parts; add information above the lines; draw arrows to show how sentences can be arranged. In short, model the revision process for them so that they understand how to mark up their own manuscripts to say what they want them to say. As you are writing, also say the punctuation marks aloud, working subtly on the concepts of the beginnings and endings of sentences.

Finally, recopy the revised story yourself on bookstock paper the size of the final book. Invite volunteers to illustrate this section.

Part II of the project is individual writing, with each child writing about a single piece of information he or she has gleaned through the unit. It may be a recipe for a treat or a description of how to milk a cow. Provide time for children to talk about what they know most about before they begin to write.

Younger children may want to draw a picture and then write just a single sentence, a caption. Second and third graders should have no trouble writing the information they know and then providing illustrations. Have students revise their drafts just as you revised the group composition on the board, marking the manuscript with needed changes. Encourage small group discussions at this point, too, and foster the spirit of helping someone else with his or her writing.

Presenting and Publishing

The class story appears at the beginning of the book, with individual pages following. This project provides a good opportunity for children to learn about the basic parts of a book, preparing a *Table of Contents* and even an *Introduction* telling the purpose of the book. This kind of project deserves to be laminated so that it can be read and enjoyed by many children—"We made a book! Let's read it again...and again." The laminated pages can then be bound together with yarn or notebook rings, providing a permanent copy that can also be studied by parents and by future classes.

Followup

More writing ideas on the theme of foods include the following:

■ Write a week's menu of healthful foods for breakfast, lunch, and dinner.

■ Learn to read the labels on the foods you find at home. Make lists of the ingredients in your breakfast cereal, macaroni and cheese, bread, pudding, lunch meat, margarine, and fruit drink. Tell other children what you learned in a Show and Tell.

■ Create a new snack treat. Test your wonderful invention on brothers and sisters before bringing it to school.

■ Learn about the kinds of foods people in other lands eat and write about them or describe them for the class.

■ Run some taste tests. Blindfold classmates and see if they can guess what they are eating. Keep records of how often they are right and wrong. Or run a soft drink challenge for yourselves and write about the results.

■ Conduct a poll of people's favorite foods—parents', teachers', the principal's. Then write a short report of your results for the class.

OUR TOWN

Many children grow up never fully realizing the richness and resources of their own community, just as many adults never fully appreciate everything their town has to offer. This unit engages students in some informal research to discover their town or city—what it is, who lives in it, how it functions, where to find things in it.

Content Objectives

This unit is intended to help children know and understand:

■ How their town or city functions: its government.
■ How their community developed and grew: its history.
■ The strengths and resources of their community: its culture, educational facilities, recreational opportunities.
■ The problems it faces: economic, social, ecological.

Writing Idea

The major writing project of this unit is a book, *A Guide to Our Town.* Each member of the class will contribute one chapter about a specific resource, problem, or point of history. Interim writing projects will include writing letters, jotting down notes from interviews and speeches, and keeping notes on reading.

Writing and Learning

Prewriting

Begin this unit by helping students discover what they already know about their city or town and what they might like to learn about it. To kick off the unit, ask children the following questions. If they know the answers, have them put these down in a notebook they will maintain for the project. If they do not know the answers, keep the questions listed on the board as a starting point for possible things to learn:

■ How old is our town?
■ How or why was it established?
■ What is it known or important for?

- Who runs our city?
- What services does our city supply for us?
- What are some problems we face in our community?
- What problems may we face in the future?
- What do you like best about living in our city?
- If you have lived in or visited other towns, what do you like best about them? What is similar or different about our town?
- What do people in our city do for a living? Do your parents or other family members work in our city? What do they do?

An excellent way to orient students toward the community and start seeking answers to their questions is to have a series of speakers or a panel discussion in which community members talk about the town and its functions and operations. Consider inviting some of the following to speak to the class:

librarian	city planner or manager
local historian	firefighter
city council representative	police officer
school board member	health official

In their project logs, students should keep brief notes and perhaps write a reaction or response after each speaker's presentation. They should also practice questioning skills, learning how to ask good questions of city experts.

After children have begun to think about the events, people, and affairs of the community, help them start thinking about questions they want to answer. What resources can they use to discover more about their town?

One excellent place to begin looking is the telephone directory where students will be able to locate many public institutions. This activity also provides the opportunity for them to learn how to use alphabetized material to find information. Whether they live in Ajo, Arizona; Bath, Maine; Peoria, Illinois; or Seattle, Washington, they will find listings for such offices and agencies as the following:

Accounting Office	Housing Commission
Assessor	Human Relations Department
Board of Water and Light	Libraries
Building Safety Commission	Mayor's Office
Cemeteries	Parking Violations
City Attorney	Parks and Recreation
Community Development	Police Department
Council Office	Refuse Collection
Emergency Offices	School Department
Fire Department	Tax Collector

In this activity, it is helpful for three or four children to share a telephone book. Teachers may be able to obtain extra copies from the telephone company or from children who can bring in a copy from home.

The Yellow Pages of the telephone book will yield further information about private businesses and services. Here students will find other aspects of their community listed—some they may have known about and many new discoveries.

As the search proceeds, have students add to a chalkboard list of questions and areas they would like to learn more about. What does a tax collector do? How expensive is it to have bumper stickers printed? What happens at an animal hospital? Then have students focus on specific questions they would like to answer for themselves. Depending on the situation, students can work alone or in pairs to find answers to these questions.

Now ask how children can find out even more information about some of the areas that seem most interesting. One of the most obvious resources they can use to discover more about their town is *people*—businesspersons, city officials, friends, and neighbors. Individuals or pairs of students can write in their notebooks the names of people who can tell more about the town.

Letterwriting. As part of the prewriting research for the guidebook, have students write letters. From the lists of resource people they have developed, help each student or pair find the names of several persons to whom they can write for more information. The class can brainstorm for questions to ask in these letters, to make certain that requests for information are stated clearly. Letters can be drafted, revised, and finally checked for spelling and mechanics. Before students prepare their envelopes or final drafts, make mockups of a standard letter form on the board for students to follow. Stamp and mail the letters (or, if postage is scarce, arrange for hand delivery, either by students or by the school delivery system).

While waiting for anwers to the letters, help children locate other resources. Teachers can sometimes obtain class sets of local newspapers free or at a reduced rate, and these are excellent resources for everything from information on local businesses to neighborhood news. Have students clip interesting articles, either pasting them in their notebooks or adding them to a file folder.

Other Resources. Draw on parents for this project. They may wish to speak to the whole class about their special areas of interest or expertise, or teachers may wish to invite them to a working session to assist students with special interests and needs. Remind children to take notes on the visiting parents' comments.

Also encourage children to watch local television news and to listen to radio news to find out more about the town. Again they should keep notes and ideas in their notebooks, which by now, will be getting rather full.

The notebooks will swell somewhat more with the addition of pamphlets, historical leaflets, travel guides, city maps, guides to services, etc. In an hour or two downtown teachers can acquire a great number of free materials to help students with their research. In addition, many correspondents will send back fliers and monographs in response to children's questions. If the school librarian also has this kind of literature on hand, students can head to the library for further reading and note taking.

Information gathering may take a few weeks. During this time have each student maintain a list of the material he or she has gathered. Also help children organize their notebooks for the safe and orderly keeping of notes, articles, letters, pamphlets, brochures. When you judge that the information gathering is sufficient, it is time for students to begin drafting *A Guide to Our Town*.

Writing and Revising

Discuss possible audiences for the *Guide* with the children. For whom do they want to write? The audience may be their parents and people living in the community, acquainting them with little-known facts; it may be younger children, telling them about important aspects of the community; or it may be strangers or visitors, telling them about the pleasures of the community. Whichever audience they choose, children should keep it in mind as they draft.

In writing "research papers," children too often copy exactly what they have read instead of digesting the information and using their own language. Students whose prewriting research has been careful and solid should not have this problem—they should know so much about their town at this point that original language will just bubble out. However, to make certain the writing is not derivative, we suggest two strategies. First, divide students into groups and have them talk through their plans before writing. This encourages them to phrase things in their own language, not that of a public relations brochure. Second, have them write the first draft of the paper without referring to their notes or other information. This may seem a little odd to them, but after they have finished the draft they can go back to their notes to look up any specific information they could not remember while drafting.

After the drafts have been completed, divide the class into small reading groups to listen to the drafts and make comments and responses. Encourage the groups to focus on the proposed audience for the *Guide*. Will the readers be able to understand the material? Has all the important information been included? Has anything been left out? Circulate among the groups during this discussion, adding questions to keep the groups on task. After the groups have completed their discussions, have students write a second draft, incorporating needed changes. Then have them make one more check for spelling and mechanics while preparing a clear, readable copy.

Presenting and Publishing

There are two basic ways to present the *Guide to Our Town*: as a one-of-a-kind book or as a duplicated book.

As a one-of-a-kind book it will be a large scrapbook. Final copies of students' writings can be pasted in, along with appropriate clippings, brochures, and letters from their research. This can be a very handsome book, displayed around the school or even in public buildings. The only drawback to this form of publication is its limited circulation, and by now the children may want to reach a larger audience.

Duplicated books can range from inexpensive spirit-copied booklets to relatively expensive offset-copied books. While you explore the possibilities, it is also a good time to begin arrangements for having students' work typed as a way of saving pages. Some teachers type children's work themselves; some use junior or senior high school typing classes; some use parent volunteers or aides. While the book is being typed, have children prepare illustrations—black ink on white paper if the book is to be offset, drawing directly on ditto masters if spirit duplicating is to be the medium. Then, after proofreading, send the master copy to the printer.

Followup

Depending on the form the book takes, teachers can either arrange to display a one-of-a-kind book or to distributes copies of a booklet to parents and local officials and businesspeople. In some cases, a sponsor, such as a local businessperson, may make large-scale distribution possible. Or, with the school's approval, the class may be able to sell printed copies at a minimal fee, creating a fund for future publishing projects or a field trip that takes students to see yet another unexplored corner of their town.

THE SEA

The sea can be examined from multidisciplinary perspectives. Artists have depicted its peace and violence; poets have created images and stories of creatures and people of the sea; novelists have told of people whose lives revolve around the sea; scientists have described the formation of the seas and their influence on the dry world; historians have discussed the effect of the sea on war and peace, trade, and the development of nations; and futurists have predicted the ways in which our lives may be increasingly interconnected with the sea. With the knowledge that such various disciplines supply, a unit on the sea could last an entire year. This project, however, focuses on a scientific/literary connection and can be a three-week unit as part of a much larger block of study.

Content Objectives

As children study the sea from various perspectives, they will learn that:

■ The undersea world is filled with fascinating and unusual life forms and with rock and mineral formations.

■ Oceans they may never have seen affect their lives and will do so even more strongly in the future.

■ People use many ways of describing what they know, have learned, and feel about the oceans.

Writing Ideas

The major writing project for this unit is open-ended, giving students a choice of writing poems or a short story about the sea. Their writing will incorporate knowledge gained during an extensive prewriting period in which they hear stories and poems, read nonfiction about the sea, and conduct a scientific experiment related to the sea. Each of the prewriting activities draws upon shorter forms of writing as well.

Writing and Learning

Prewriting

Literature about the sea is abundantly available in most school and public libraries. Throughout the unit, then, provide children with a literary perspective on the sea by reading to them daily. Include both fiction and poetry, with at least one short novel to be read over a period of a week or a week and a half. The director of the library or media center may have some suggestions, or teachers may have their favorites. Two excellent collections with sea poems are

> *One Hundred Story Poems* selected by Elinor Parker (New York: Thomas Y. Crowell, 1951)

> *The Illustrated Treasury of Poetry for Children* edited by David Ross (New York: Grosset and Dunlap, 1951).

Good novels for class reading are

> *The Sea Egg* by Lucy M. Boston (New York: Harcourt, Brace, Jovanovich, 1967)—a realistic novel about sea life.

> *Moominpappa at Sea* by Tove Jansson (New York: Avon, 1977)—a fantasy of creatures who move from their valley to an island and must learn to adjust to the sea.

After reading to the children from these or other books, allow time for them to discuss the poem or story. In addition, let them talk about the sea-knowledge in the story—the facts provided about the horseshoe crab or the white whale, for example. (Note: Be certain the information being discussed is fact, not fantasy.) Throughout the reading and discussion, let children build on both their scientific knowledge and their appreciation of literature by writing in their journals for a period of time after each reading. The journal entries can be free associations, listings of facts, reactions and responses to characters in a story.

While the whole group readings are in progress, also start children reading nonfiction on an individualized basis. Allow them to choose a book from the school library, the public library, or from their books at home. The following list is merely illustrative, intended to show the range of topics for third to fifth graders to explore:

> *The Sea Around Us* by Rachel Carson (Simon and Schuster, an adaptation of her classic book for adults). Topics include The Gray Beginnings, The Surface of the Sea, The Changing Year, The Sunless Sea, Hidden Lands, The Long Snowfall, The Birth of an Island, The Shape of Ancient Seas, Wind and Waters, Rivers in the Sea, Moving Tides, The Global Thermostat, Wealth from Salt Seas, and The Encircling Sea.

The Mysterious Undersea World by Jan Leslie Cook (National Geographic Society). Topics include Wind, Waves and Tides, The Edge of the Sea, Coral Reef, Undersea Adventure, Sunken Treasure, Ocean Depths, Miniature Oceans.

All About the Sea by Ferdinand C. Lane (Random House). Topics include How the Sea Began, How the Sea is Divided, The Rise and Fall of Continents, Mountains Under the Sea, The Unseen Pull of Sun and Moon, On the Watery Trail of the Fish, Birds That Love the Spray, Farming the Sea, Mining the Sea, Sailing the Seas, How the Seas Control Our Climate.

After children have finished reading their books (perhaps with time for silent reading in class), have them write short reviews in their journals or on four-by-six-inch index cards, In addition to the title and author of the book, have them write a short paragraph telling the information they found most surprising, intriguing, or fascinating. This writing can be used in three ways: (1) to provide a check for teachers to keep track of when children have completed reading their books; (2) to provide a set of notes for children to use in giving an oral report to a small group of students; (3) to provide an information file of individual journal pages and index cards for use by the entire class.

As a final phase of this extended prewriting period, divide children in pairs or threes to conduct their own scientific experiment related to the ocean. One good source for experiments is *Science at Work: Projects in Oceanography* by Seymour Simon (Franklin Watts, Inc.), but most libraries will have several other sources. Most of these projects involve "kitchen science," with little equipment beyond bowls and jugs, salt, and perhaps a toy boat required for success. However, if you can take the children on a field trip, so much the better; they might do some of their research at a nearby lake or river or visit a public aquarium to continue their learning.

After completing the experiments, students should jot down their ideas in an informal laboratory report in their journals. In the first section of the report have them list step-by-step the processes they followed in conducting their experiments; in the second part, have them report what they discovered. Also have them write freely in their journals about personal reactions and responses.

Writing

By now ideas for writing should be frothing about in the children's heads like tides in the Bay of Fundy. They will have experienced the sea through several perspectives: literature, nonfiction reading, hands-on scientific sharing, and their own writing in journals. It is now time for them to write, to incorporate their knowledge of the sea into their own piece of imaginative writing.

Start a brainstorming session, possibly jotting down the ideas on the chalkboard. Make certain that all ideas are accepted with equal enthusiasm, because the purpose is to generate a wide range of possibilities. Encourage children to think of adventures, romances, mysteries, and science fiction. Since their knowledge of the sea will be incorporated in their stories, they may want to think of ocean-related settings for stories: in a submarine, on a fishing boat or ocean liner, in a surfer's shack in Hawaii, in an underwater city in the year 3000, in a fishing town in Maine. The central conflicts of their stories will probably center around oceanic problems: sea creatures dying off, an island sinking, a ship under attack by pirates while sharks circle, a leak in the underwater city. Their characters also will probably be nautical: ship captains, seamen and women, tradespeople, residents of strange and exotic ports.

Poets can consider various forms for their work: story poems, limericks, haiku, image poems, and shape poems.* Their work may focus on telling the tale of a sunken treasure, creating a series of word pictures capturing the beauties of the deep, or making an ode to whales, fishermen and women, or seashells.

Also have children discuss whom they would like to have as the audience for their work. They can consider writing for other classes, younger grades in the school, or for parents and relatives. Deciding on the audience will help lend focus to their work.

Writing and Revising

After children have brainstormed for possible topics, have them pick a topic and write. (If two children choose the same topic, it is no problem; the stories or poems will turn out differently and also provide interesting material for comparison.) Encourage them to share their ideas with one another while they work and to ask questions of you if they have problems. When they have completed their first drafts, have them read these aloud in small groups of three or four for suggestions on ideas, structure, wording, and so forth. Also encourage students to ask questions of one another that will let

---

*If these forms are not familiar, see the Teachers and Writers Collaborative publication, *The Whole Word Catalogue* (New York: Macmillan, 1978), which describes many different simple poetic forms.

the writer know whether he/she is communicating clearly or needs to clarify any part of the draft.

Copyediting and Presenting

Before students recopy their drafts into final form, help them check for spelling and mechanical errors. First have them search for errors in their own papers; then let them exchange with one or several classmates to get additional eyes searching. Finally, teachers may want to spot proofread some of the papers to make certain students are receiving the help they need.

The revised and copyread poems and stories can then be copied on good paper, possibly with illustrations added. These "illuminated" manuscripts can then be displayed for other students or parents.

Followup

Some additional topics on The Sea are as follows:

■ Write a poem or a series of poems describing sights you encounter on a sea voyage.

■ Create a description of an imaginary underwater world and describe the lifestyle there. What do people eat and wear? How do they spend their time?

■ Write an imaginary diary describing life stranded on a desert island.

■ Describe what you think is a major problem involving the sea—pollution, for example. Write an editorial or a letter to an editor outlining your solution to this problem.

■ Write an advertisement that would help convince people of the need to protect the sea against misuse.

■ Write a newspaper article about a famous historical event that occurred on the sea (such as the defeat of the Spanish Armada by the British). Or write an imaginary diary from the point of view of someone who participated in that event.

■ Write a pirate's log or journal for a month.

■ Examine sea animals, either from books, a classroom aquarium, or a visit to an aquarium. Write a poem or a series of poems about these beasties. Or write about what you think it would be like to be a sea creature.

■ Design a one-person submarine that would be yours and yours alone, to take anyplace you wished. After drawing the design of the sub, write about your life under the sea.

■ Write a story describing how you think the seas came into being.

NORTH AMERICAN INDIANS

This unit immerses students in a culture unlike their own so that they may broaden their understanding of other ways of life and of different cultural expressions through art, music, religion, economics, architecture, and so on. It provides for group or collaborative writing as well as individual ventures.

Content Objectives

■ To learn about and appreciate the contributions of various North American Indian tribes to U.S. culture.

■ To study specific modes of cultural expression and to understand how these modes express a lifestyle.

■ To avoid the stereotypes of North American Indians promoted by television, movies, and other mass media.

■ To understand current issues related to North American Indians today.

Writing Ideas

Provide students with a number of writing/researching options for this project, including the following:

■ Read about the life of a particular tribe of Indians in North America, then write a story about an Indian child showing the relationships among family members and each person's contributions to the household. Or write a report in the form of a diary of a young Indian showing his or her family relationships. Give the family authentic names and use as many Indian words as you can. You may wish to create a chart that illustrates family living units for the bulletin board.

■ After listening to records of Indian music and reading some Indian poetry, try your hand at writing Indian chants and poems. You may also wish to look into books on Indian crafts to create instruments to accompany your chants and poems. Or make a collection of original Indian poetry and your own creations in a bound book.

■ Research Indian food. Find out what members of a particular tribe ate, how they grew or acquired it, how they prepared it, and how they served it. Make a recipe book giving the history of the recipes. Create and serve your classmates an Indian meal (substituting household ingredients for any of the Indians' ingredients that are not easily available).

■ Recreate an Indian ceremony. Learn about the special occasions the Indians celebrated and what they did at their ceremonies. Explore costumes, art, music, dance, and facial and body makeup. Present an Indian ceremony for your class, using homemade costumes and your own music and art. Provide small booklets or an information sheet explaining the history and meaning of your ceremony.

■ Study Indian names of towns, cities, states, mountains, rivers, and lakes, especially names of places close to where you live. Make a dictionary of Indian place names in your area.

Writing and Learning

Prewriting

Obviously this unit depends on the availability of a good supply of resource materials on North American Indians: books, recordings, perhaps films and filmstrips. Before beginning the unit, check with the media center director who may be able to arrange a book cart for your room or set aside a library shelf for students' use.

Several of the projects are suitable for small groups of students as well as for writers working alone. The advantage of the collaborative work is that students can teach and learn from each other. They can provide a sounding board for helping each other make decisions about the information they need, when they need more, what to do when they have it, and how to improve the work when it begins to take shape.

The initial step in the prewriting stage is for students to delve into the materials to discover ideas for their project. Teachers can devote several reading periods to free reading in the books available, then encourage students to focus their ideas, picking a specific project and narrowing their topic to a particular Indian tribe. Students should keep informal notes or logs on their reading, and they will need instruction in a very simple form for bibliographic entries for keeping track of the books they have studied; for example:

Frank Willis, *The Chippewa* (Alma, Mich.: Heritage Press, 1968).

Groups collaborating on projects should meet frequently to see how their pool of material is coming along. Students planning to write alone can also meet as a group or with the teacher to make progress reports. The teacher's principal responsibility at this stage is *seeing that the work gets done.* This means helping students who are having trouble locating resources, helping students record necessary bibliographic information, helping students decide what information to write in their notes, and helping students who are stalled or confused by a surfeit of information.

As a final stage in prewriting have students make ordered lists of the main points or ideas they want to cover in their project. These lists should be quite specific, giving as many details as possible, because they will serve as a rough outline for drafting. (Note: This is not a *formal* outline, but something that provides enough focus for students to write a clear and organized draft.)

Writing and Revising

Students working in groups will probably want to split their topic into parts, with each person writing one part. In the Indian ceremonies project, for example, this would mean one person writing about costumes, another about holidays, a third about makeup, a fourth about dance steps. As they write, either alone or in groups, students should feel free to confer with one another and with the teacher. Questions about whether or not their writing is clear, interesting, specific enough will occur at this point.

After each person has a rough draft (and the groups have pooled their writing to make a common draft), have students work in pairs or groups to read one another's work, making suggestions for improvement. Provide some guide questions for them to answer about the content and form of the writing:

> *Content.* Is the writing clear? Do you know what the writer is talking about? Do you need more information? What would you like to know more about? What confuses you? In a few sentences, summarize for the writer what you learned from his/her draft.
>
> *Beginnings and Endings.* Does the draft catch your attention early and keep it throughout the paper? Does the ending let you know that the writer has ended in an interesting way?
>
> *Summary.* Describe *one* thing you think the writer could do to make this paper better.

47

Sometimes the answers to these questions will lead students to do further research. And, of course, they should get some ideas from their peers that will help them with the rewriting. The teacher's advice should be very useful during this stage—most importantly, modeling behavior that shows the kinds of comments that are appropriate as responses.

After students have finished their revision, it is time for the final polishing. With the help of their peers and teacher, they should correct spelling, punctuation, and capitalization.

Final Copy and Presentation

Because this unit offers several different options, the preparation of final copy will vary from group to group, individual to individual. The group recreating an Indian ceremony, for example, will place most of its emphasis on an actual performance, with the public writing as a handout or booklet explaining customs. The group preparing an Indian meal will prepare copies of its recipe book and bring real food for the meal itself. Other students will write booklets of poetry and make charts of Indian lore and culture. Although providing students with choices of topics can sometimes make class-work seem complicated, teachers will also find at this stage that work on a diversity of projects creates a great deal of interest in the class, as students will be eager to find out about the work of other groups.

On the day of the presentation of projects, if everything has gone well, you may wish to invite parents or other classes to the performance.

Followup

The possibilities for additional content-area writing on North American Indians are numerous. Among the projects that can be suggested to students to extend the unit are the following:

■ Study a tribe from a particular geographical area. Describe how the features of that region affected the lives of the Indians who lived there.

■ Investigate the roles of Indian men and women. Make a bulletin board display showing how roles of men and women today compare with the roles of the tribe you studied.

■ Write a short story about the confusion of an Indian child from the past who is propelled into the present and modern U.S. society.

■ Pretend you are a reporter. What questions would you ask of an Indian who lived 300 or 600 years ago? Write a dialogue; find a partner; rehearse; then tape record the interview.

■ Pretend you are a famous Indian from the past. Write an account of an important incident in your life. Or write a letter to present-day Americans sharing your ideas on an issue of importance to you.

■ Create a bulletin board that shows a map of the largest or most interesting or most powerful or longest-surviving Indian tribes. Put as much information on the map as you can, while making it readable and appealing.

■ Study various kinds of Indian houses and create some models. Write descriptions of their construction to accompany your display.

■ Study Indian games. Write a set of rules for several different games and then teach your classmates to play them.

Part III

Applications and Extensions

SUMMARY OF PRINCIPLES

1. Keep content at the center of the writing process, addressing yourself to *what* the writing says, allowing *how it says it* to be treated incidentally.

2. Make certain students know their material before writing: content understanding shines through in student writing.

3. Design writing activities that help students structure and synthesize their knowledge, not merely regurgitate it.

4. Provide audiences for student writing, real or imaginary, so that students have a sense of writing for someone other than the teacher.

5. Look for writing activities that allow the student to play the roles of *learner* and *researcher*.

6. Teach the *process* of writing:
   a. Spend much time with prewriting, helping students acquire a solid grasp of the material.
   b. Provide assistance and support as students write, helping them solve problems as they arise, rather than waiting until they turn in the paper.

7. Let students revise one another's papers. Provide support through revision checklists and guidelines.

8. Don't confuse revising with copyediting:
   a. Teach revision first, having students clarify the content and substance of their work.
   b. Turn to copyediting of spelling, mechanics, usage, etc., only in the final phases of writing.

9. Display or otherwise publicize student writing through shows, demonstrations, book publishing (duplicated or one-of-a-kind), oral readings. Don't be the only reader of your students' work.

10. **Keep content at the center of the writing process.**

FINDING TOPICS

"What can I write about?" is students' perennial lament. The teacher's variation of that theme is, "What shall I have them write about?" That teacher concern helps explain the popularity of books that provide laundry lists of topics and ideas for youngsters' writing, inviting the teacher to pick a topic virtually at random for the next writing assignment. We prefer a more systematic approach to writing and content teaching and think that if students are to grow as both writers and learners, there has to be some rhyme and reason to the sequence of topics they study.

We have discovered that if teachers take the sort of interdisciplinary approach described in Parts I and II of this book, topics for writing and learning appear everywhere. Each day something happens at school or in the world at large that lends itself to content writing—"Wouldn't it be interesting to have students write about *that*?"

For the newcomer to writing in the content areas, the textbook—whether science, social studies, mathematics, or other subject—provides the logical place to start the search for topics. Each new chapter in the book provides a source of potential writing ideas.

In discussing textbooks, however, we need to mention one of our biases quickly: most of the reading, writing, and discussion topics supplied by commercial textbooks are poorly designed. Textbook writers violate most of the principles of content-area teaching we have described. Too often the topics stress memorization and regurgitation; they seldom build in any provision for an audience; too often they lead to "homework writing" that is boring to write and read.

Some of those topics can be salvaged, however, by simply applying good content-writing principles. For example, a science book presents the following as a "study assignment":

> Write a report on the ingredients contained in a number
> of common household products and how they work.

Such an assignment invites bad writing because it seems aimless, without focus, and lacking in audience. We would rewrite it something like this:

> Make a search of the cleaning cabinet around your home
> or apartment—the place where all the cleaning supplies
> are kept. Choose two or three products that are used

around your home regularly—detergent, rug shampoo, floor wax—and copy the ingredients from the label. Then, based on your study in this unit, write a paragraph or two about each product, explaining to your parents (or whoever uses the products) just why they work as they do.

Another assignment in the same book reads simply:

Write a report on the life of Niels Bohr.

Instead, the teacher can say:

I've brought in a number of biographies of famous scientists (including Niels Bohr). I'd like you to read one of them and then do some writing about the person's life. Don't just summarize what the person did; instead choose an important moment in that person's life and write a dramatic scene (or short story) about it. We'll act them out (or read them aloud) to the class.

Thus a number of textbook concepts can be covered through interdisciplinary writing. Further, teachers will find that if they adapt textbook topics in this way, their students will learn the material more successfully than they have in the past.

Curriculum guides, although little more than listings of fundamental concepts to be covered at each grade level, can often supply ideas for content-area writing. To convert one of these concepts to writing ideas, look for "the literacy connection" and ask yourself, "How can that concept best be expressed through writing?" Then return to Part I of this publication, "A Primer on Teaching Writing in the Content Areas," and develop the concept as a writing topic.

The daily newspaper is filled with potential ideas for content-area writing. While browsing through the paper, teachers can often find news stories that are immediately relevant to their planned content teaching for the day. The news stories, in turn, can lead to writing that ranges in complexity from a simple journal response to daily events to a full-scale inquiry-centered unit on a key issue or topic of the day.

Similarly, newsmagazines can provide a wealth of ideas for content-area writing. The science or education or medicine or world events sections of such periodicals will probably not only contain ideas for writing, but some prewriting resources as well.

Other popular magazines can provide a starting point for writing in the content areas. English teachers discovered years ago that by talking to the local paperback/magazine distributor, they could often arrange to have out-of-date magazines supplied to their classes at no cost. Other teachers can probably arrange to receive magazines from *Ranger Rick's Nature Magazine* to *Popular Photography* in their classrooms at more or less regular intervals. These specialized magazines, in turn, can trigger the development of interdisciplinary writing lessons and units.

Learn to look for the real-world connection between what you are teaching (and what students might write about) and events in the school neighborhood, the community, and the state. Issues and concerns of day-to-day living have a tendency *not* to be easily classifiable by discipline. Therefore study of an issue such as ecology, or town planning, or the water supply will naturally cut across many disciplines in the humanities, sciences, and vocational fields. And writing, in turn, underlies all of these areas.

James Beck, a teacher at the University of Wisconsin, Whitewater, has his college students systematically look at how different disciplines view common issues and problems, forcing them to take an interdisciplinary perspective.[2] We tried this same idea with a group of Michigan teachers, exploring the topic of The Elderly from as many different points of view and from as many different interdisciplinary perspectives as possible. We reprint their list *in toto* just to show how exhaustive such a list can be and how easy it is to develop one.

THE ELDERLY

Science

■ How old do various animals live to be? Which animal has the longest lifespan? Which one has the briefest lifespan? Prepare a chart or display showing these relative lifespans.

■ What happens to cells when they grow old? Why don't we continue to grow new cells forever? Read about the aging of cells or conduct experiments and present your findings.

■ Do you share any of your grandparents' personality or physical traits? Interview your parents and study family photographs to discover resemblances. How do these come about? Prepare a photo-display to prove your points.

■ Read about or interview a doctor on lifelong eating habits. What does your eating style determine about the length of your life?

■ Explore cryogenics and the possibility of freezing sick people and reviving them later when cures for their diseases are known. Present your findings in a report or possibly a realistic science fiction story.

Mathematics

■ How many people are alive on planet earth now? How old are they? Design a world map showing population centers and the approximate percentages of people in various age brackets.

■ Trace the increasing average life expectancy in the United States from colonial times to the present. Prepare a display or a talk showing what has happened. What does science/mathematics project to be the average lifespan 50 or 100 years from now?

■ Formulate a year's budget for a person over 65 taking into account social security benefits. How difficult is it for an elderly person to get along financially in retirement?

■ Explore the statistics on food production in the world today. Where does the world's food come from? Who consumes the most food? Who eats the least amount? Prepare the copy for a television or radio program that explores some of the problems of world hunger.

Art and Music

■ Study the photographs of the elderly in *The Family of Man*. What did the camera "see" in these people? Translate your impressions into words.

■ Read the biographies and autobiographies of artists who were still creating late in life: Picasso, Casals, Toscanini, O'Keeffe, Nevelson. What kept them going? Prepare a class presentation on some of these artists.

■ Study the ways in which the elderly are portrayed in paintings. What clues does a painter provide to show that a person is old? Then make some photographs of older people. Are the artists correct?

Social Science

■ Prepare a report on the various social care programs for the elderly: social security, medicare, medicaid, retirement plans. Write a position paper or editorial on the subject.

■ Investigate how different countries and cultures take care of the elderly. Then prepare an evaluation of such care in the United States.

■ Write an imaginary scene between a person who is about to enter a home for the elderly and his or her son or daughter. How does the elderly person feel? How does the "child" feel?

■ Find out if there is an adopt-a-grandparent program in your community and begin corresponding with a person in a home for the elderly.

History/Social Studies

■ Research the American Indian treatment of their elderly and write a monograph or report for the class.

■ Visit a home for the elderly and conduct a series of interviews with residents about what life was like during their youth. Use this information to compile a study of a period in twentieth century U.S. history.

■ Put yourself in the role of a person who lived in an earlier era and have him or her visit our society today. What would, say, Eleanor or Franklin Roosevelt think about the modern-day United States? What would George Washington think? Present this as a dramatic monologue for the class.

■ Locate an elderly person who is practicing a dying art or craft. Ask the person to teach you the basics of the craft, and use the ideas in an article, perhaps with photographs.

Civics

■ Research the history of the Gray Panthers, a group of advocates for the elderly, and describe their plans and programs.

■ Invite your local state representative to speak to the class describing current legislative proposals concerning the elderly. Write questions for the legislator to answer, and after the program, write letters to him or her describing your position on the proposed laws.

■ Research the laws and regulations concerning the establishment of homes for the elderly. What kinds of permits and credentials are required? Analyze these requirements. How do these rules and regulations protect the elderly?

■ Try to find out why U.S. senators are frequently elderly men, older than obligatory retirement age for most people. Are these men wiser than the rest of the population? (Similarly, study the age of various U.S. presidents. Can an elderly person be a successful ruler of a country?)

■ Do you think the elderly should have a right to die when they wish? Study the question and write a pro and con discussion, airing both sides of the issue. Then describe your own position. (Or study the subject of *euthanasia*, mercy killing, and write a similar paper.)

Vocational/Career Education

■ Learn about careers for the elderly and write a guidebook that would be helpful to an older person, about to retire, in finding something interesting and worthwhile to do.

■ Look into careers that involve the elderly: being a gerontologist (doctor for the elderly), running a community recreation center, and so forth. Prepare a display showing these career choices and giving their qualifications.

■ Interview an elderly person, perhaps one of your grandparents, on his/her feelings about working and a career. How do people feel about various kinds of work after spending a lifetime in such activity?

■ What is "lifelong education"? Where does one get it? What is important about it? Can you see yourself being involved in lifelong education after you have finished school or college?

Other Subjects and Disciplines

■ *Athletics.* Write a booklet describing various sports and other athletic activities that the elderly can enjoy.

■ *Technology.* Study *bionics*, the science of "mechanical" replacement parts for the body, and write a description of how this may affect aging during your lifetime.

■ *Futurism.* Consider the effects of research into DNA and the possible production of antibodies to protect the aged from diseases.

■ *Religion.* What do some elderly people you have interviewed believe about life after death? How have their attitudes changed as they have grown older?

The list can go on and on. Depending on the makeup of the class, a selected half-dozen or more of these topics can create a solid unit lasting several weeks. A broader selection can yield interesting activities stretching over a month or more.

But for those who would like additional suggestions for topics, one more list follows.

MORE IDEAS
FOR CONTENT-WRITING PROJECTS
IN THE ELEMENTARY GRADES

Ears: Human, Animal, Fish
Islands
Deserts
Desserts
Medicine Men and Women
The Telephone
Wolves
The Olympics
Eggs
Fires and Firefighting
Stars
The Instruments of
   the Orchestra
Baby Brothers and Sisters
Dogs, Cats, and Other Pets
Insect Languages
Colonies: Human and Animal
Flight
Photography
Egypt
China
Time Capsule
Habitats
Typewriters
Saving a Life
Oil Painting

Venomous Reptiles
The Changing Climate
Clothing
Rivers, Lakes, and Streams
Factories
Railroads
Hats
Buildings: Who Designs Them?
Buildings: Who Builds Them?
Ice Cream
Holidays
Songs from Around
   the World
Questions About Science
Questions About Numbers
Questions About People
Questions About Places
Questions About Events
Puzzles
Africa
Soviet Union
The Family
Transportation
SCUBA Diving
Video Games
Making Models

EVALUATION AND GRADING
OF CONTENT WRITING

We have stressed the value of peer revision as an essential part of the writing process (see Part I). Although this helps dramatically reduce the theme-correcting burden, the fact remains that most teachers feel a need to make some comments, either written or oral, about student papers. As noted elsewhere, we suggest focusing the comments on *content*, stressing "writing" only as it affects the clear presentation of that content. These comments, then, should include such considerations as whether or not the paper successfully communicates the basic ideas, adequately defines terms, and is easily understandable to the proposed audience. Most research in writing suggests that at this stage, praise is far more helpful than criticism, and the most useful comments are those that not only point out things well done, but explain to the student *why* they were well done.

Grading is one form of evaluation that teachers must also deal with. It may be tempting for the teacher interested in writing in the content areas to give a double grade: one for content and one for writing quality. We recommend against this practice—although acknowledging its popularity among teachers—because it creates an unnecessary schism between writing and content. Instead, we suggest that the teacher apply content criteria—Are the facts right? Are the observations sound? Is the message accurate?—and focus on writing only as it enhances or detracts from the content. Thus the teacher can lavish high praise (and a good grade) on a paper that not only presents sound information, but does so articulately and even artistically. Likewise, if a paper is sloppily revised and carelessly spelled, the author should know that poor writing interfered with comprehension and resulted in a lower grade.

Grading should be relatively easy and painless if an assignment has been carefully designed and explained to students. In the course of prewriting, students will discuss what it is they are expected to include in their papers and the audience for their writing. The time spent on prewriting, then, is actually the beginning of the evaluation process. Further, if the teacher monitors their progress throughout the drafting, revising, and copyediting stages, students will have received considerable advice informally. The final grades in such assignments should therefore come as no great surprise to anyone.

An even better approach is to place writing on a pass/fail or credit/no credit basis. This eliminates pressure about grades and allows both student and teacher to concentrate on the quality of the writing and the content material. In a P/F or Cr/NCr system, minimum standards must be clearly articulated, and students must know that the teacher will not automatically accept any piece of writing they submit. In our experience with these systems, we have always used "best effort" as a measure: if students feel they have given their best work, and if we, as teachers, intuitively feel they have, then we accept a paper.

In a related kind of grading, the contract system, papers are similarly given credit/no credit, with the total number of papers submitted as a guide to the final grade. Despite an inherent weakness of emphasizing quantity over quality, the contract system works well if standards and criteria of evaluation are stated clearly.

It is crucial for teachers of writing in the content areas to recall that *grading* is not the same as *evaluation*. Although we believe the impact of grades on student writing should be minimized (or eliminated if possible), this is not to say that student writing should not be evaluated. Much of the evaluation should come through the peer group revising and copyediting sessions—where young writers get a real sense of how their writing affects real readers. But the teacher obviously must enter into the evaluation process, too. Sometimes this can be done through written comments on papers, which is time-consuming. Another method is the miniconference conducted on the spot—a minute or two spent in class discussing a part or all of a paper. Evaluation also comes when students submit their writing to public scrutiny by publication or display or oral reading to a group of peers or adults. It is unfortunate that grades too often substitute for these more substantial forms of evaluation.

Traditionally, writing evaluation has given most emphasis to mistakes and errors in content, mechanics, and usage. It is important to emphasize that students learn both writing and subject matter best when they *succeed* at what they have set out to do and when someone helps them understand why they have succeeded. Thus, in responding to and evaluating student writing, be lavish with praise for things well done rather than despairing of students' writing failures. Itemizing every fault on a student paper seldom produces positive growth and can be destructive of morale and self-confidence. This is not to imply that one should spare the rod and spoil the child. If a paper fails to communicate successfully, a student ought to know it. But, to use another cliche', nothing succeeds like success.

In the end, the best evidence of the success of a student's writing (or the success of a writing program) is in the writing itself. We strongly recommend that teachers initiate a *portfolio system* for maintaining copies of student writing (including notes and drafts, if they are of interest to the teacher). Such portfolios, carefully maintained for a semester or a year, provide evidence of student growth, in content mastery as well as in writing. Further, portfolios can provide useful material for discussion with parents and for conferences with individual students. A portfolio is better than an individual paper for diagnosing a student's writing problems and seeking solutions. And it can be handed along to teachers at the next grade level to provide some continuity of both content and writing instruction from one year to the next.

Some schools and districts may be interested in creating evalua-

Tchudi

tion programs for all their students; in this age of accountability, a number of such systems have been developed. Usually they involve collecting writing samples on a pre- and post-test basis, after which teachers work in teams either to assess the writing *holistically* (making impressionistic judgments about such qualities as form, structure, style, and correctness), or to evaluate *primary traits* (searching for particular characteristics of good writing). Faculties engaging in such programs often report a greatly increased awareness of the importance of writing and of the strengths and weaknesses of their students' writing. For a detailed description of these approaches to schoolwide evaluation, as well as practical teaching pointers on the whole question of theme grading and evaluation, see Maxwell and Judy.[11]

CONTENT WRITING
ACROSS THE CURRICULUM

There are, it seems to us, few limits to what can be accomplished by a single classroom teacher pursuing a content-area writing program for part or all of a school year. But it is self-evident that if students are to see writing as something valuable in all their schoolwork (and in later life), they must encounter interdisciplinary writing regularly, from kindergarten through twelfth grade. They must use writing as a tool for discovery and expression in all their subjects and come to understand or intuit its usefulness in any learning situation. With this in mind, a number of schools and districts in the United Kingdom, Canada, and the United States have begun developing something generally titled "A Policy of Writing Across the Curriculum." Evolved through faculty meetings and workshops as well as through in-service sessions, such policy statements outline each teacher's responsibility for developing writing skills. (Most statements are, in fact, broader than writing and include reading in the content areas as well. However, this discussion, will be limited to writing.)

We will not attempt to outline such a policy in this publication, because any statement must be hammered out and agreed upon by the people who will implement it. That task is not easy, for by no means do all teachers share the assumption that writing (and reading) must be a schoolwide concern. A statement, then, must take into consideration the concerns of teachers who feel they cannot teach writing successfully or who dismiss it as the responsibility of someone else—next year's or last year's teacher. Nor can the expectations in a policy statement be perceived as unreasonable by the cooperating teachers. Although it is quite practical for youngsters to do a bit of content writing in every class every day, to suggest it as a quota or even as a desirable goal may result in protests and the breakup of a writing-across-the-curriculum discussion.

Nevertheless, we do want to provide teachers with a model for a writing curriculum policy statement and then suggest how a school or district can go about implementing one.

At the elementary level, writing across the curriculum is made a bit simpler because of self-contained classrooms and the fact that teachers in most schools teach most, if not all, subjects. Some elementary schools, however, are departmentalized. Still, language arts skills are frequently isolated from subject matter teaching even in the self-contained classrooms, so the policy statement would address itself to the following concerns:

■ That elementary teachers make an effort to include one good, solid content-writing project in every subject-matter unit they teach.

■ That informal, short writings be used frequently, even daily if possible, in support of instruction, so that students keep notebooks, journals and diaries, research logs, observations, sketches, and responses to their studying and reading.

■ That a wide range of writing forms be practiced so that elementary school children explore the full range of possibilities for writing in the content areas, imaginative as well as expository.

■ That evaluation of writing in the content areas focus not only on what is said but how it is said, with teachers emphasizing that in all areas, writing quality is important along with learning facts and concepts.

The four previous statements are concerned with writing in individual classrooms, but the policy statement should also focus on articulation between grade levels, suggesting:

■ That each teacher collect a representative sample of the students' content writing to pass on to the next grade level.

■ That teachers meet yearly at a minimum to discuss how they are teaching content writing at their grade level and to propose ways of making writing growth sequential and reasonably orderly from grade to grade.

■ That teachers establish a file of content-writing activities as a way of avoiding duplication of effort and sharing successful strategies.

■ That teachers demonstrate the success of the program by conducting an annual content writing fair, similar to a science fair or talent exhibit, to display the best of the year's writing.

And so forth. In most cases, the elements of the policy statement will become clear just as soon as a group of elementary teachers get together with a commitment to do something about writing.

In the end, no writing-across-the-curriculum policy statement will reflect a perfect or total consensus. Some teachers may regard the whole enterprise as a waste of time and refuse to participate; others may file away the policy statement and ignore it. But it has been our experience that schools willing to make the effort to develop the policy often find the writing program improved dramatically. Most faculty members will make an effort to adhere to the policy and to make it work. The amount of writing done in a school will quadruple, at least, and students in all classes will become more excited about and involved with their written work.

Some other suggestions for launching a writing-across-the-curriculum policy:

■ Include parents in the planning, letting them express their concerns about the quality of their children's writing. Also invite parents to participate in the literacy program, especially by serving as tutors or even as volunteer theme readers.

■ Start a pool of lesson plans and teaching ideas in the content areas as a catalyst for reluctant or cautious teachers.

■ Treat writing as a focus for in-service training for a year. Bring in writing consultants from a university or another school district and have them work on a long-range basis, helping develop the program, not simply making one-time presentations and departing.

■ Issue press releases on the concern for literacy to notify the community of the school's commitment.

■ Set up an annual school writing awards program.

■ Create a buddy system in which good writing teachers help subject teachers plan writing activities and consider ways and means of developing good lessons. (In exchange, subject teachers can help language arts teachers locate good subject matter materials for use in the English content-area writing program.)

■ Conduct an annual school- or systemwide writing week, in which students in all classes, elementary as well as secondary, focus on a common theme through writing. Present this writing and project work at a school- or districtwide writing fair. Invite parents and the media—they will love it.

Selected Bibliography

1. Abruscato, Joe, and Hassard, Jack. *Loving and Beyond: Science Teaching for the Humanistic Classroom*. Pacific Palisades, Calif.: Goodyear Publishing Co., 1976. Excellent source of inquiry-centered writing and speaking in science.
2. Beck, James. "Theory and Practice of Interdisciplinary English." *English Journal* (February 1980): 28-32. An overview of how teachers can survey interdisciplinary resources on any topic.
3. Bogojavlensky, Ann Rahnasto and others. *The Great Learning Book*. Menlo Park, Calif.: Addison-Wesley, 1977. Numerous interdisciplinary projects, both fun and educational.
4. Delmar, P. Jay. "Composition and the High School: Steps toward Faculty-Wide Involvement." *English Journal* (November 1978): 36-38. Practical pointers on ways and means of getting faculty involved in writing programs. Applicable at middle school, junior high,and elementary school levels as well.
5. Edwards, Pat. "101 Ways to Publish Student Writing." In R.D. Walshe, ed., *Better Reading, Better Writing, Now*. Epping, New South Wales: Primary English Teaching Association, 1977.
6. Elbow, Peter. *Writing with Power*. New York: Galaxy, 1981. The bible of books on small group and peer revising of papers, filled with practical suggestions for the classroom teacher.
7. Heck, Shirley. "Planning: The Key to Successful Interdisciplinary Teaching." *Kappa Delta Phi Record* (April 1979): 116-21. Describes a branching, individualized planning procedure for interdisciplinary units.
8. Judy, Stephen. *The ABCs of Literacy*. New York: Oxford University Press, 1980. Analyzes the current writing crisis and suggests steps parents and educators can take to ensure that students can write in the content areas.
9. Judy, Susan, and Judy, Stephen. *Gifts of Writing*. New York: Scribner's, 1980. Describes numerous ways of publishing and presenting youngsters' written works.
10. Lehr, Fran. "ERIC/RCS Report: Promoting Schoolwide Writing." *English Education* (Spring 1982): 47-51. Surveys content-area writing programs.
11. Maxwell, Rhoda, and Judy, Stephen. *Evaluating a Theme*. Rochester, Mich.: Michigan Council of Teachers of English, 1979. Also available from ERIC/RCS, 1111 Kenyon Rd., Urbana, IL 61801.

12. McLuhan, Marshall and others. *City as Classroom*. Agincourt, Ont.: Book Society of Canada, 1977. Explores numerous interdisciplinary probes into "media" like *money, lightbulbs,* and *computers* that affect our lives without our knowing it.

13. Ruchlis, Hy, and Sharefkin, Belle. *Reality-Centered Learning*. New York: Citation Press, 1975. Presents a method for interdisciplinary units that center on real-world topics of concern to students.

14. Springer, Mark. "Science in the English Classroom." *English Journal* (October 1976): 35-36. A junior high school teacher explores possible interrelationships between science and literature.

15. Summerfield, Geoffrey. *Topics in English*. London: Batsford, 1965. A classic book on the project approach to teaching.

16. Wurman, Saul, ed. *The Yellow Pages of Learning Resources*. Arlington, Va.: National Association of Elementary School Principals, 1972. How to use the telephone book to generate interdisciplinary learning projects.